IF YOU LOVE ROBOTS, YOU COULD BE...

By May Nakamura   Illustrated by Natalie Kwee

Ready-to-Read

SIMON SPOTLIGHT

An imprint of Simon & Schuster Children's Publishing Division
New York   London   Toronto   Sydney   New Delhi
1230 Avenue of the Americas, New York, New York 10020
This Simon Spotlight edition May 2020
Text copyright © 2020 by Simon & Schuster, Inc.
Illustrations copyright © 2020 by Natalie Kwee
For information about special discounts for bulk purchases, please contact Simon & Schuster Special Sales
at 1-866-506-1949 or business@simonandschuster.com.
Manufactured in the United States of America 0320 LAK
2 4 6 8 10 9 7 5 3 1
ISBN 978-1-5344-6523-7 (hc)
ISBN 978-1-5344-6522-0 (pbk)
ISBN 978-1-5344-6524-4 (eBook)
Library of Congress Catalog Card Number 2020932242

Glossary

Artificial: made by humans

Artificial intelligence: the ability of a robot to act, and appear to understand, like a human

Electricity: a kind of energy that can travel through wires to power a robot, lightbulb, or other device

Engineer: someone who uses math and science to design and build machines and equipment

Machine learning: the science that allows a robot to change the way it behaves and grow smarter by learning from information it gathers on its own

Machinist: someone who makes the parts in machines like robots

Program: to write instructions for a robot in a code that computers can understand

Prostheses: artificial body parts made by humans to help assist or replace a weak or missing body part, such as an arm or a leg

Robot: a machine that can move on its own and complete difficult tasks

Robotics electrical engineer: an engineer who develops the robot's power and sensor systems

Robotics mechanical engineer: an engineer who builds the robot's physical body, and often designs the parts inside it

Robotics software engineer: an engineer who uses computers to develop the robot's software, which acts like a brain

Sensor: a device that provides information about its surroundings, such as sounds, smells, or sights

Software: a set of instructions and information programmed for computers that tells a robot what to do

Note to readers: Some of these words may have more than one definition.
The definitions above match how these words are used in this book.

CONTENTS

Introduction

Do you love robots?
Isn't it amazing that
robots can walk, talk, fly,
go to space, and more?

Did you know that some people get to make robots as part of their jobs? When you grow up, you could help make robots like they do!

Chapter 1:
Robotics Mechanical Engineer

What exactly is a robot?
Robots are machines that are made
by people. Robots can move
and complete tasks on their own.
They often do things that might be
hard, boring, or dangerous
for humans.

People who make robots as part of their jobs work in the robotics (say: row-BAW-ticks) business. Many of them are engineers (say: en-juh-NEERS) who use math and science to design and build things like machines.

A robotics mechanical engineer (say: mih-KAN-nih-kull en-juh-NEER) is in charge of creating a robot's body and the parts inside it.

First, they decide what parts
the robot needs to do its job.
If its job is to pick up a bottle,
it needs parts for a robotic hand
to hold the bottle,
an arm to lift it up, and more.

They must think about each part's shape and size, and how the parts will fit together.

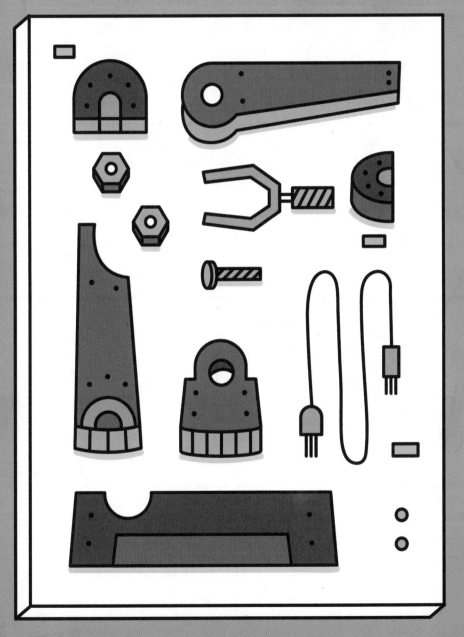

They decide how each part
will look and give drawings to a
machinist (say: muh-SHEE-nist)
whose job is to build the parts.

After putting the parts together, the engineer does tests to see if the parts fit, move well, and do what they are supposed to do. If needed, the engineers make changes and test again.

Mechanical engineers have to be patient. It often takes hundreds of tests before all the parts finally work!

If you want to be a mechanical engineer, ask a grown-up to help you take apart an old toy or clock that has moving parts, so you can see how it works. What kind of robot would you like to build someday?

Chapter 2:
Robotics Software Engineer

Even if a robot has a body,
it needs a computer inside for it
to know what to do and how to do it.
The computer is like the robot's brain.
It is how a robot dinosaur toy knows
how to roar, and how other robots talk
and tell jokes!

The computer contains software, which is a set of instructions and information for the robot.

Robotics software engineers program, or write, those instructions in a code that computers and robots can understand.
In a way, software engineers make the robot's brain!

Some robots have software that
makes them able to act like humans.
This ability is called artificial
(say: art-tuh-FIH-shull) intelligence.
Artificial means "created by people."

Artificial intelligence is how
robots know when to smile
or ask how someone is feeling.
It makes them seem more like people
instead of machines.

Software engineers also program some robots to become smarter on their own by using information they learn after they are built. This is called machine learning.

Robot dogs that don't use machine learning can't learn who their owner is. A robot dog that uses machine learning can learn and remember its owner's face, voice, and more.

Over time, the robot dog might
be trained to wag its tail when its
owner says its name!
It can also keep learning . . .
a lot like a real dog!

If you want to be
a software engineer,
you can learn computer skills
by reading books or taking classes.
What would you like to program
a robot to learn or do?

Chapter 3:
Robotics Electrical Engineer

Just like you need food and water,
robots need power to move around
and do their jobs.
A robotics electrical engineer
(say: ih-LECK-trih-kull en-juh-NEER)
works on systems that power robots!

Some robots get their power from electricity, an energy that can be stored inside batteries.
The electricity travels through wires and other devices
to power the entire robot.

Electrical engineers also work on the robot's sensors (say: SEN-sirs). Sensors are devices that give robots information about what is happening around them. It is similar to the way that eyes and ears give humans information about sights and sounds.

Some robots are programmed to "sleep" until their sound sensor notices someone saying their name, and then they "wake up."

Some electrical engineers also work on robotic prostheses (say: prahs-THEE-seez). Prostheses are artificial body parts that some people with missing or weak body parts choose to use.

Robotic prostheses can do things standard prostheses usually can't. This is because they contain special sensors that can receive signals from the user's body.

If someone uses a robotic leg, the sensors can tell if they want to bend it, and then trigger a motor to make the leg bend.

Electrical engineers must be good at sharing ideas and working with other engineers.

If you want to be a robotics electrical engineer, you can look for a nearby robotics team for kids and compete in robotics contests. You'll learn to make robots together!

Engineers are still learning many new things about robots. It is an exciting subject that grows and changes every day.

Someday, you could create awesome robots that help people around the world!

Robotics mechanical engineer, software engineer, and electrical engineer are just a few of the cool careers for people who like robots. Turn the page to discover even more!

More Cool Robotics Careers!

An **animatronic technician** (say: an-nuh-muh-TRAH-nick teck-NIH-shun) builds puppet-like robots used for entertainment. The robots might appear in theme parks or on movie sets.

A **machinist** makes metal parts for robots and other machines. They use a lot of tools like drills, saws, and grinders.

A **robotics research scientist** studies and experiments with new kinds of robotics technology. They develop new ideas about robots and their uses.

A **robotics technician** makes sure robots are running smoothly in places like factories. They follow instruction manuals to set up and repair robots.

A **rover driver** sends instructions to a rover, which is a robotic vehicle in space. They tell the rover what to look at and where to go.